To Marguerite Jukes—
for hosting all the Ladies' Business Club meetings
of my childhood, whether she wanted to or not.
I love you, Mom!

XOXOXOXO

Acknowledgments

Thanks to Sonia Bledsoe, M.D. for thirty-five years friendship, ideas and inspiration.

Thanks to all the doctors who reviewed the work upon which this book is based (*It's a Girl Thing: How to Stay Healthy, Safe, and in Charge*).

Thanks to pediatrician Vicki Papadeas, M.D. for medical review of *Growing Up: It's a Girl Thing: Straight Talk About First Bras, First Periods, and Your Changing Body*.

Thanks to all the editors who've contributed insight and advice throughout the process—but special thanks to Nancy Hinkel, for expert editing and endless patience.

GROWING UP

IT'S A GIRL THING

STRAIGHT TALK ABOUT FIRST BRAS, FIRST PERIODS, AND YOUR CHANGING BODY

by **MAVIS JUKES**

illustrations by **Debbie Tilley**

Alfred A. Knopf 🐕 New York

A Note to the Reader

The information in this book was gathered through careful research by the author. The content was carefully reviewed medically. Information in the area of children's health is continuously changing. If you have questions about anything in this book, please talk to your pediatrician.

THIS IS A BORZOI BOOK PUBLISHED BY ALFRED A. KNOPF, INC.

www.randomhouse.com/kids

Library of Congress Cataloging-in-Publication Data
Jukes, Mavis.
Growing up: it's a girl thing: straight talk about first bras, first periods,
and your changing body / by Mavis Jukes ; illustrations by Debbie Tilley.
p. cm.
Includes index
Summary: A guide for pre-adolescent girls to the changes that puberty brings to
their bodies, including information about menstruation.
ISBN 0-679-89027-0 (pbk.) — 0-679-99027-5 (lib. bdg.)
1. Menarche—Juvenile literature. 2. Menstruation—Juvenile literature.
3. Girls—Physiology—Juvenile literature.
[1. Puberty. 2. Menstruation.] I. Tilley, Debbie, ill. II. Title.
RJ145.J85   1998
612.6'62—dc21   98-18113
Printed in the United States of America
10 9 8 7

Contents

About this book

Sometime after about age eight—or even before—a girl will begin to notice changes in her body. Bumps appear behind her nipples. One by one, hairs show up under her arms. Pubic hair begins to cover the private place between her legs—in front. These changes signal the beginning of what is called *going through puberty*. And going through puberty is what this book is about.

Sooner or later every girl will have breasts, underarm hair, pubic hair, and will begin her period—because every girl goes through puberty. Not every girl begins at the same age, though. Some girls begin as early as age eight, or even younger. Many are happy and excited about the changes. Others feel embarrassed and wish their bodies would just stay the same.

No matter when a girl begins to go through puberty, she will still be a kid. Having breasts and hair in private places and having a period won't change that. She will not be a woman for a very, *very* long time.

She will not be expected to act like a grownup and will not be treated like one.

Are You Ready?

Do you feel ready to read about breasts, bras, periods, pads, underarm and pubic hair, perspiration and deodorant? Do you feel ready to learn about what these changes have to do with *human reproduction* (people growing up and making babies together)?

If you're not sure, ask a parent or teacher to help you decide if it's a good time for you to begin reading this book.

Chapter 1

My Mom and Me

❧ The Ladies' Business Club

When I was in elementary school, I grew two small breasts. At about the same time I sprouted a few hairs—not many—in a special place. Once these breasts and hairs made their appearance, I felt private about my body and didn't let anybody see me naked.

Secretly I felt these new additions to my body were beautiful. And I was right.

Before I undressed to take a bath, I locked the bathroom door. Then I made sure the little hole somebody had accidentally poked in the bathroom door was filled with a blob of toothpaste.

While I was running water into the tub, I checked the size of my budding breasts. They were small. I would look under my arms in the mirror to see how many hairs were there. There were just a few.

In the bath I would borrow big handfuls of shampoo bubbles from my head and make two piles on my chest. This would help me to see how I would look one day when I was a woman with huge breasts.

I would soap my body and practice writing my name in cursive on my belly. Then I'd draw—maybe a heart or a flower. When I got out of the bath and dried myself, I would fluff up my pubic hair to make it look fuller. I would smear a little blob of my mom's cream deodorant under each arm.

I knew all the basic things about womanhood because of my mom. We had a club: the Ladies' Business Club. The club had two people in it: my mom and me. Meetings were held whenever I felt like it and were always held in my mom's bathroom or bedroom, but never when my parents were there together—only when my mom was there alone.

The rules were that I could come in when she was taking a shower or bath or going to the bathroom—but she had to stay out when I was doing any of these things.

Those were club rules; I made them up and my mom followed them.

But just in case club policy might have slipped her mind, I locked the bathroom door.

Most mornings my mom took a shower. But sometimes she'd just give herself a quick sponge bath. Naked, she filled the sink and washed her armpits, crotch, and rear with a soapy washcloth. She rinsed herself, carefully wringing out the washcloth, often humming a tune.

It was fun to hang out with her when she was bathing. We'd chat about this and that.

A few days each month, when my mom had her period, after she had bathed and dried off, she would climb into a thin elastic belt with two little metal clasps on it. She turned it around so there was one clasp in the front and one in the back. Then she hooked a big white pad onto the clips.

Next she put on a garter belt. Then she put on cotton underwear and pulled the garters, which were attached to elastic ribbons, down through the leg holes. She attached stockings, which had seams up the back, to the garters. (Pantyhose hadn't been invented yet.)

My mom bent over when she fastened her bra, so her breasts were in the right place in the cups of the bra when she stood up. Then she dabbed on some cream deodorant and rubbed it in.

She then pulled a slip over her head and put on a blouse and buttoned it. She stepped into a skirt and zipped it up the side. She put on high-heeled shoes. Then she brushed her hair. Finally, she put on perfume and lipstick, earrings, and beads or a pin.

Later on, if I happened to cruise into the bathroom when it was

3

time for my mom to change her pad, she wouldn't seem at all embarrassed. She would just sit on the pot, busily tending to the project.

I would watch with interest as she unhooked the pad from the elastic belt, front and back. She never tried to hide the blood on the pad.

She just rolled it up, wrapped it in newspaper, and threw it into the trash.

Then I would hand her a new pad from the box in the bathroom cupboard. She would attach it to the clasps on the elastic belt. Sometimes she would sprinkle on a little deodorant powder, which came in a tin can. She'd stand up, haul up the belt so the pad was snug against her body, pull up her undies, wriggle down her skirt, flush the toilet, and march out.

Not all moms feel as comfortable sharing their privacy with their daughters as my mom did when I was a kid. It's not necessary or important for every mom to give every daughter permission to walk in and out of the bathroom, and most moms prefer to be left alone while going about their private business. Just like most girls do.

But just because something's private doesn't mean it's secret. It's reassuring to talk and think and read about things to do with growing up.

Welcome to the Ladies' Business Club!

Chapter 2

Feathers and Blossoms, Breasts and Bras

❀ Popping the Question

Almost as soon as my breasts began to grow, I wanted a bra. I was willing to wait for a garter belt and stockings, high-heeled shoes, and an elastic belt with a fluffy white pad attached. But I wanted a bra and I wanted it *now*—whether I needed it or not.

The problem was I was too shy to ask my mom.

I would practice asking the question over and over again to myself.

I would stand beside her in the evenings after supper and dry all the dishes, thinking I might at any moment turn to her and say, "Mom? Can I have a bra?"

But the words didn't come.

Finally, one day my mom and her friend Agnes were sitting on the front porch in chairs with flowered cushions, drinking iced tea. I stood in the doorway, kicking open the screen door and stopping it from banging shut again with the toe of my shoe.

"Do you want something, sweetie?" my mom asked.

"Yes," I told her through the screen. "I want a bra." I hurried back in the house and sat on the edge of my bed and blushed. How embarrassing! Had I actually asked for a bra? Right in front of Agnes?

The next day my mom and I went to a small clothing store on Main Street. With the help of a saleswoman, we chose the only bra that was available in my small size.

I went into the dressing room alone and pulled the curtain closed tightly, so nobody could peek. I took the bra out of its small box, which had a picture of a girl about my age on the front. The bra was white, with a tiny pink flower in the middle and a fake pearl in the center.

The bra smelled so new and delicious!

I leaned over to put it on the way my mother put her bra on. This wasn't really necessary, since I was still practically flat. I struggled to hook the little metal clasp in the back. I looked in the mirror and fixed the straps so the cups of the bra wouldn't look so empty. I turned to the side and then to the front again.

I put on my shirt and carried the box out of the dressing room.

My mom paid, and we left as though nothing in particular had happened. But what a great secret it was to be wearing a bra.

I could hardly wait to tell everybody about it!

❀ Breast Buds

At some point after about age eight—or even before—a girl will notice bumps behind her nipples. The bumps mean that her breasts are beginning to develop.

Sometimes a girl develops a breast bud on one side first. If this happens to you, don't worry. Breasts take a few years to grow to their full size, and they don't have to begin growing at the same time in order to end up about equal in size.

Breast buds are one of the first signs that a girl is beginning to go through puberty.

❀ What Is Puberty?

Puberty is the name for a set of changes that happen to our bodies between the ages of about eight and about sixteen. The changes happen on the inside and on the outside. Our *emotions* (feelings) are also affected.

These changes are caused by *hormones*. Hormones are chemicals produced inside our bodies. They are like tiny messengers. They give signals to parts of the body that work together to make us able to *reproduce* (make babies). The signals cause this system to begin to work.

> Girls who begin changes early sometimes feel "different" from the other girls. If you're beginning to go through puberty before your friends are and feel like it's hard to be first, talk to your mom or another trusted adult about these feelings. Sharing feelings with those we trust can be very comforting.

❖ Pubic Hair

A friend of mine told me that she was in the shower, lathering up, when she noticed her daughter peering at her from around the edge of the shower curtain.

"Mom?" asked the little girl. "When I grow up, will I have feathers, too?"

Pubic hair begins to grow at about the same time that breast buds form. It begins as a fuzzy patch that thickens and spreads out, carpeting a small area between our legs in the shape of an upside-down triangle. Pubic hair can be curly or straight, black, brown, red, or blond.

We're not sure what purpose it has other than decoration!

❖ Underarm Hair

Hormone messengers not only cause breast buds and pubic hair to appear but also cause hair to grow under our arms, in our armpits.

After a while, we have a tuft or small carpet of hair under each arm. The hair can be black, brown, red, or blond, curly or straight. It doesn't keep growing and growing like the hair on our head. It just grows to a certain length and then stops.

As our underarm hair begins to appear, we also usually notice that the hair on our legs has become thicker and sometimes darker.

Chapter 3

Information, Please

❀ Shaving

It's perfectly natural to have hair on legs and under arms, and there's no need to shave it. Many girls and women leave it just as it is.

But others do shave it off.

Once it's shaved off, it grows back again.

If you want to shave the hair from your legs, underarms, or both, please get permission first. Ask for a demonstration if you haven't already had the chance to watch.

Don't shave facial hair or pubic hair. It grows right back and will feel stubbly. And itchy!

❀ Electric Razors

Some women shave with electric razors. They carefully buzz them under their arms and up and down their legs—usually between the ankles and the knees.

Electric razors and other appliances that plug into a power outlet in the wall are not meant to get wet and should never be used near water. It's possible to get *electrocuted* (shocked to death) by touching a plugged-in appliance that's wet or touching one when you are wet or are standing in water.

Certain *battery-operated* electric razors are designed to get wet. They say "wet/dry" or "fully submersible" on them. If an electric razor doesn't have these words on it, **don't get it wet**.

Special Alert

If an electric appliance, such as a hair dryer or electric shaver, does get wet, don't go near it or let any other kid go near it. Get help from an adult.

✿ Disposable (Throwaway) Razors

Disposable, or throwaway, razors are popular and fairly safe to use.

A good time and place to shave with a disposable razor is while taking a bath in the bathtub. The area to be shaved needs to be wet and slick, so the razor can move smoothly over the skin. It helps to use soap, shaving cream, or gel.

✿ It doesn't take much pressure to shave hairs off, so it's not necessary to press hard. The razor's edge should be rinsed occasionally.

✿ It's not a bad idea to wait a few minutes before putting on deodorant after shaving. Otherwise it may sting.

Razors should not be shared. It's easy to get nicked or cut while shaving. Germs that might be present in the blood of one person can be spread if the person gets blood on the razor from a nick or cut and then shares it with someone else.

✿ Odor

At about the same time that underarm hair grows, people begin to *perspire* (sweat) more freely under the arms. Armpits get damp and smell musty when people get hot or while exercising.

If we bathe often enough, we don't need to worry about this.

The smell of sweat under arms is natural, but many people choose to cover up the odor with a *deodorant/antiperspirant*. Deodorants/antiperspirants are sold in grocery stores and drugstores and other shops. They come in different forms—spray, cream, stick, gel, and roll-on. They all work pretty much the same. Some are scented and some aren't.

People who use deodorant/antiperspirant put a little under each arm in the morning or after a shower or bath.

There's no need to put it on after bathing at bedtime.

❀ Growing Up Just Plain Includes Smelling Stronger

… than before puberty begins. But bathing regularly and wearing clean clothes take care of this.

If for some reason you don't have the chance to jump into the shower or bath as often as you'd like to, you can give yourself a sponge bath with warm water, a little soap, and a washcloth.

Do as my mom did in the Ladies' Business Club: First wash your armpits, then rinse. Then wash your crotch and rinse carefully. Last, wash your rear, then rinse. Don't reverse the order. The rear should be washed last because the germs that are there need to stay in their own area!

And while we're on the subject, girls and women should wipe from front to rear when we go to the bathroom. This prevents germs from sneaking from our rear over into our *vaginal area* (the place between our legs close to where pee comes out), where the germs can multiply and cause infection.

When you bathe, beware of perfumed products, including lovely little perfumed soaps, bubble-bath products, bath beads, and other good-smelling things developed for use in the bathtub. Many girls and women find that their skin is just too tender for these products. They can be especially irritating to the soft, sensitive skin in the vaginal area.

If you do try perfumed products, start by using just a little—and make sure you rinse well.

✿ More About...Hormones

Besides giving signals to the body to begin growing breasts and pubic hair, hair under the arms, and thicker hair on the legs, hormones are responsible for lots of other changes.

Hormones can cause *acne*—otherwise known as pimples, blemishes, and zits. Many girls (and boys) get acne when they go through puberty.

There are acne medicines available in drugstores that can be wiped onto the skin, and there are special soaps available that help control acne. If your skin breaks out, your parent can help you choose one.

Your doctor may *prescribe* (write up a special order for) medicine for acne or may suggest that you visit a *dermatologist* (a doctor trained to treat skin problems) for advice.

Please don't use medicine without your parent's permission. Read and follow all directions carefully.

Chapter 4

More About . . . Breasts

Breasts come in lots of different shapes and shades and sizes: large, medium, small, very small, dark, pale, full, flat.

Nipples are the spots in the middle of the breasts. We're all born with nipples, and their appearance changes when we go through puberty. Nipples also come in different shades and sizes. Some are brown, some are plum-colored, some are dark pink, some are pale pink. The different colors of our nipples go along with the different shades of our skin.

Some nipples cover a large area of the breast. Others cover very little.

Sometimes a few hairs grow out of the dark area around the nipple. The hairs are normal. You may also have tiny bumps (*glands*) around the nipple. These are normal, too.

Both the hairs and the bumps should be left alone.

You may notice when you're cold that your nipples temporarily change in size and shape. This happens to everybody!

✿ We're One of a Kind

Some girls worry that their breasts will end up being too small or too big. But there's really no one way breasts are "supposed" to look. Breasts are beautiful, big or small, dark or light, round or flat.

Many of the women models in bra or swimsuit ads in magazines have medium-size or large, pale, round breasts, but that doesn't mean most women do.

Whatever size and shape your breasts turn out to be when fully developed, they will be right—for you.

✿ Breast-feeding

Breasts can produce milk after a woman has a baby. The baby drinks the milk by sucking on the mom's nipple. This is called *nursing* or *breast-feeding*.

When a baby nurses, the mother feels a gentle tugging feeling. Normally it doesn't hurt, unless the baby has teeth and decides to take a nibble!

Breast-feeding is very healthy for babies and usually is a wonderful experience for both baby and mom.

But not all women breast-feed their baby. In some cases the mom's body doesn't produce enough milk. Or the baby might not be a good nurser. Or the mom just may not want to breast-feed. So the baby drinks a special kind of milk designed just for infants called *formula*.

Chapter 5

Bras

Not every girl is as happy about having a bra as I was. Lots of girls put off getting bras because they don't want to wear one.

Some women don't want to wear them either—and don't! Lots of people around the world go braless. There's certainly no law that says we have to wear one.

The main work of a bra is to support the breasts. What this means is this: Bras help hold breasts up. Many girls and women feel more comfortable when their breasts are held snugly against their chests, especially when running, jumping, dancing, playing hopscotch, working out, jumping rope, and playing sports.

Without some kind of support, breasts and nipples can be seen moving around under a shirt, and some girls and women don't like to show that.

A bra provides privacy against peeking when a girl has on a sleeveless shirt and also helps to keep nipples from showing through a thin shirt.

Did you know that making comments or teasing about breasts in a bothersome way is against the law? It is a kind of *harassment*. Tell a parent if this happens—and also tell your teacher or principal if it happens at school or on the school bus.

❧ Bra Choices

The good news is that there are many different styles of bras, so all of us who wear bras can find one we're happy with. Some bras are fancy, some are plain. Some hook in front, and some hook in back. Some snap or zip closed.

Some look and fit like tank tops or workout gear. The material they are made of is stretchy and strong. These are called *sports bras*. Lots of girls and women choose this style of bra.

Bras made of soft, stretchy material are comfy and allow for growing. These are great, especially for first bras. So are sports bras, if you exercise or play actively. Sports bras should not be so tight that they cause a lot of pressure on your breasts.

Some bras have bendable wires covered with fabric

front hook bra

strapless bra

underwire bra

sports bra

sewn in under the cups. These are called *underwire* bras. Some women feel they're uncomfortable; others like them.

Do you want a bra with a clasp in front? Or in back? How about no clasp? How about wide straps instead of thin ones?

The answer is: You probably don't know.

And you know what? You don't need to know. You don't have to know about every kind of bra to choose your first one.

As long as a bra fits comfortably, it'll work just fine. When you're growing, you might need to change your bra size pretty often, and this will give you the chance to experiment with different styles and discover what bra suits you best.

❧ *Shopping for a Bra*

When it's time to get a first bra, most girls will have a mom, step-mom, foster mom, grandma, aunt, or big sister to give advice—but not all girls will. Some girls go with a friend and a friend's mom. Some girls go with a dad, and some dads even know how to help shop for a bra.

But Dad might not have a clue where to begin in a storeful of racks of bras that clasp in front or hook in back, have underwires or don't, are sports bras or aren't.

Still, he can provide support by standing around looking at the ceiling or sitting in a chair and discreetly saying nothing while a girl shops with the help of a saleswoman.

I have a friend who picked her first bra completely on her own. She selected a strapless bra trimmed with rabbit fur—a bra fit for the Queen herself.

She was delighted with the bra and still remembers it fondly—but I forgot to ask if she ever tried to do jumping jacks in it.

If you pick your own bra, think about comfort and what's practical. A bra that's too tight or too loose is very annoying to wear. Since bras are worn next to the body, they need to be sturdy enough to be washed often.

So steer clear of rabbit fur trim—it doesn't wash well. And for everyday use choose a bra with straps! Strapless bras are designed to be worn with gowns, other low-cut clothing, or shirts and dresses with skinny straps. They have a habit of inching down or sliding down and continually need hoisting or hauling back up. This is all just about as much fun as having underpants that ride up and cause wedgies all day long!

A good way to begin to shop for a bra, whether by yourself or with a friend or family member, is to find a saleswoman and ask: Where are bras for preteen girls?

This will narrow down the hunt.

❧ Fitting a Bra

People come in many different shapes and sizes, so there are many different bra shapes and sizes.

Some bras, like some sports bras, for example, might just be labeled *small, medium,* and *large.* These are pretty easy bras to fit. Just try on a few and choose the size that's the most comfortable.

❧ Number-Letter Bra Sizes

Many bras are labeled with a number and a letter that tells us a very particular size. The *number* tells us how big around the bra is when it's fastened, and the *letter* tells us how much room is in the cups.

When we shop for one of these bras, we don't have to worry about how tall or short we are. Only two measurements matter: How many inches are we around the chest—measured just below our breasts? And how many inches are we around the chest—measured across our nipples?

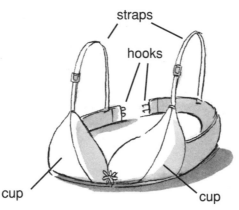

straps

hooks

cup

cup

Bra-Measuring Tips

Measure around your chest just below your breasts. If you measure an even number, such as 32—add four inches to find your *number* size. You will probably find that size 36 will fit, because 32 plus 4 is 36.

If you measure an odd number, such as 27, then add five inches to the number to find your number size. You will probably find that a size 32 will fit, because 27 plus 5 is 32.

You also need to know your *letter* size (cup size). Measure again—this time passing the tape across your nipples.

If the measurement across your nipples is the same number as it is below your breasts, your letter size will probably be AA or AAA.

If it's one inch bigger, it will probably be an A.

If it's two inches bigger, it will probably be a B.

If it's three inches bigger, it will probably be a C.

If it's four inches bigger, it will probably be a D.

If it's five inches bigger, it will probably be DD or DD/E.

It isn't necessary to be naked on top to measure for a bra. Measurements can be made with a shirt on, as long as it's not too thick. Someone in your family or a friend can help you. Or you can measure yourself.

Specially marked measuring tapes are available in most stores that sell bras.

In many stores saleswomen have been specially trained to measure for bra size. If you don't want the saleswoman to measure you, say so. Just ask to borrow the tape measure, and you can go into a dressing room and measure yourself.

❁ Or . . . you can just guess!

Take a few bras into the dressing room. Pick one size 32A, one size 34A, one size 36A, and one size 38A *in the same style*. Try them on, and you will get a general idea about what number size you should be looking for.

Cup too big? Try a smaller one—AA. Cup too small? Try a B. You'll figure it out!

In the smallest size range there may be only one or two choices of styles and fabrics. In sizes 32A and up, there is usually a large selection, including colors and prints.

Find the cup size that you feel happy with. How does it look with your shirt on? If the cup size is too big, the cup will look wrinkled. If the cup size is too small, it won't comfortably cover your breasts, and extra "bulges" may appear.

Every bra company has a slightly different idea of size. You may need to spend a while in the dressing room choosing a bra that seems right for you. Many bras have adjustable straps; some have little clasps in the back that can be fastened to make the bra fit a *little* looser or a *little* tighter. It's fine to experiment with different adjustments.

Tip: An easy way to put on a bra that hooks in the back is to put the bra on around your *waist* with the hooks in the front, near your belly button. Fasten the hooks. Then whirl the bra around so the hooks are in the back and wriggle into it.

Remember:

Number and letter sizing is just a guide, not a guarantee that the bra will fit. It's a good idea to try on a bra before you buy it. If for some reason you can't or don't want to try it on in the store, *remember to leave all the tags on* when you try it on at home, and keep the *original bag* and the *receipt* so that if you're not happy with the fit, the bra can be returned or exchanged.

Questions about a store's return policy for bras or other things?

Ask before you pay.

❀ *Washing a Bra*

Many bras, especially fancy ones and ones made of special fabrics, should be washed by hand or else in the *delicate cycle* of the washing machine, in *cold or warm water*.

Please ask permission before using the washing machine. Check the label on the bra for washing and drying instructions. Most bra labels will say "no

bleach" or "no chlorine bleach." *In any event, it's not safe for kids to use bleach or other household chemicals without adult supervision. If something needs bleaching (whitening), ask for help from a grown-up.*

To wash a bra by hand, fill a sink partway with warm or cool water. You can use hand soap, a little liquid dish soap, or a little detergent used to wash clothes in the washing machine.

Not sure what soap is right? Ask an adult, or else just use the bar of soap your family uses to bathe with.

Wash the bra, rinse it well, and hang it up. Or lay it on a towel to dry. Most bras will dry overnight.

❀ Padded Bras

Many girls and women adore having smallish breasts and aren't interested at all in having their breasts look bigger.

But some girls and women long for bigger breasts.

Some bras and swimsuit tops are padded—to make breasts appear larger than they really are. Sometimes the pads are removable. In the old days these were called "falsies" or "removable bra inserts."

Sometimes the padding is designed to lift the breasts and create "cleavage" (the upper part of the breasts, which can be seen when some women wear a swimsuit, gown, or low-cut blouse, shirt, or dress). These are called "push-up bras."

❀ Sallie's Bathing Suit Disaster

When my friend Sallie was a kid, she went to summer camp. One year she decided she was sick of waiting for her breasts to grow bigger. So she secretly helped herself to her mom's removable foam rubber bra inserts and hid them in her suitcase.

At camp she tucked the bra inserts into her bathing-suit top and walked to the pond where the kids were swimming, supervised by the lifeguard—a cute teenage boy.

Sallie strolled up and tested the water with her foot.

Then she took a running leap off the dock into the water.

She kicked her way up to the surface and blinked the water out of her eyes. Then she noticed that her mom's two very bright white foam rubber bra inserts had popped out of her suit and set sail across the lake.

She took a deep breath and ducked back under the water, reappearing some distance away among the lily pads at the edge of the lake.

She saw the lifeguard skimming her mother's bra inserts from the lake with a long metal pole with a net on the end.

"Well, now," he called out. "Who would these belong to?"

The other kids swam closer to look.

"Whose on earth are these?" the lifeguard kept calling out.

Sallie silently lurked among the lily pads, watching and saying nothing.

Padded bras! Who needs 'em? Breasts are beautiful—big or small.

Maybe yours will be a whole generation of girls who "just says no" to padded bras!

Chapter 6

IT'S MY BODY

Your body belongs to you and always will.

Breasts are so special and beautiful! Yours belong to you and you alone. They're part of your special private territory and always will be. You are the boss of your breasts—*and* the rest of your body.

✿ Staying Safe and in Charge

Grownups who are in love with each other often express their loving feelings *sexually* (by romantically kissing, holding, and touching each other in ways that feel good). This showing of affection can include touching each other's private places. This kind of sexual touching is permitted only when both people agree to it—and either person can change her or his mind and say no at anytime.

Showing affection sexually is for grownups only, and should never involve a child.

❀ It's just plain NEVER okay...

...for an adult, teen, or older child to *intentionally* (on purpose) try to touch or rub up against any private places on a child's body for a *sexual* reason. On a girl, the private places include her breasts, her upper inner thigh, her *vulva* (crotch), her bottom, and her *anus* (the place where poop comes out).

Anyone who says it's okay for a grownup or teen to have sexual contact with a child is *lying*.

And it's not just touching that's against the law.

Here are some other examples of behaviors that are also not allowed: Showing a kid photos of an adult's private places; asking a child to touch a private place on another person; asking a child to *pose* for photos or videos in certain positions that *display* the child's private places for a sexual purpose.

> Family photos or videos that show things like a toddler romping with a rubber ducky in the bathtub or a little kid skinny-dipping in a play pool aren't considered inappropriate. It's a time-honored tradition for families to document the shenanigans of their little children, who sometimes just naturally happen to be nude!

❧ Most adults will protect children and never harm them, ever.

Only a certain few adults (and teens or preteens) have the problem of wanting to make sexual contact with children. They are called *pedophiles*, or *child molesters*. Child molesters try to keep their problem a secret from responsible adults, because they don't want to get in trouble.

A child molester can be young or old, rich or poor, male or female—but they're usually adult males or teen males. And they're usually known to the children they try to *molest* (harm).

We want our children to feel secure and protected.

We don't want kids to feel suspicious or afraid of the people who care for them. However... it's necessary for kids to know that child molesters are sneaky and that they sometimes gain the trust of responsible adults who don't realize what they're up to!

Occasionally, a child molester is in a position of power or authority.

It isn't likely, but it is possible, that a coach, childcare worker, teacher, religious leader, club leader, camp counselor, neighbor, family "friend," or even a family member is a child molester.

> Sometimes it's necessary for a doctor, nurse, or other health-care professional to check out private places on a kid's body, and this is perfectly fine, provided that there's a medical reason (injury, irritation, illness, checkup, or other health concern) and provided that it's done with the parent knowing about it and giving permission.

✿ Trust your feelings.

It's possible for a kid to sense that something is wrong without understanding what it is. Listen to your instincts.

Kids almost always have a feeling that something is wrong when an adult teen or older kid tries to "get sexual." That's because something *is* wrong. A child should trust his or her gut feeling and say no! Then tell a responsible adult what happened, right away.

> If you or anyone else is in immediate danger of being harmed, call **911** or dial "0" for the operator and ask to be connected to the police.

Remember:

The kid can **NOT** get in trouble for telling what happened. It is **NEVER** considered the kid's fault.

✿ Talk about your feelings.

Talking about your feelings with grownups who listen to you helps keep you safe.

Tell a parent or other responsible adult if any person or situation makes you feel uncomfortable, uneasy, confused, scared, sad, or ashamed. If the bad feelings involve a family member, tell another adult family member or other responsible adult.

Don't keep secrets from your parents.

If someone tells you to keep a secret from your parent, it is a signal that the person may have done something wrong—or may be planning to do something wrong. Tell right away.

What if a sister, brother, or friend tells you a secret about being molested? Tell a responsible adult, even if you promised you wouldn't.

Who might be the "responsible adult " a kid could tell?

A responsible adult a kid could tell might be an adult family member, a teacher, a school counselor, a school principal, a doctor or nurse, a friend's mom or dad, or any other grownup that the child feels she or he can talk to.

Or a kid could call the:

CHILD HELP U.S.A. HOTLINE

This is a special telephone number kids or grownups can call with any kind of question or concern about a child being threatened or harmed in any way by anyone at anytime.

The line is open day and night.

The call is free.

It doesn't show up on a phone bill.

It can be called from any phone—even a pay phone.

The people who answer are all trained professionals who can and will help.

The number is **1-800-422-4453.**
The easy way to remember it is: **1-800-4-A-CHILD.**

For the hearing impaired, the number is: **1-800-222-4453.**
The easy way to remember it is: **1-800-2-A-CHILD.**

X O X O X O X

Please be confident that regular old kisses and hugs and squeezes and cuddles, love pats, back rubs, rubbing noses, cozy snuggling during naps or snoozes…all are fine and healthy ways for family members and friends to show affection for children and for children to show affection back.

It's good to show affection and love in these ways and other appropriate ways, *as long as a kid feels fine about it.*

And kids don't need to worry or fret about times when people innocently brush up against, bump into, or tumble with each other during sports, games, or other playful situations—even if a private place accidentally gets touched.

These are just normal everyday events.

Chapter 7

Onward!

✿ Having a Period: What's It All About?

If you haven't wandered into the bathroom when your mom or stepmom or foster mom or big sister or grandma or aunt has been changing a *pad* or *tampon,* or if you haven't talked to anybody about *having a period,* there's something you need to know right away: Having a period is perfectly normal and healthy.

Periods usually begin when a girl is between the ages of nine and sixteen—most commonly starting at about age thirteen. Only girls and women have periods—boys and men don't.

Menstruating and *menstruation* are two other words that mean "having a period."

When a girl begins her first period, it means that her *reproductive system* has begun to work. A girl's reproductive system refers to the parts of her body that work together to make it possible for her to produce a baby someday. *A girl's reproductive system begins to work years before she is actually ready to be a mom.*

During a period, a small amount of bloody fluid—just a few

tablespoons—trickles out of the body. The place where it comes out of the body is very close to the place that *urine* (pee) comes out. This place is called the *vagina*. (More about the vagina on page 34.)

The bloody fluid is released from the *uterus,* which is inside the body. The uterus is a small, soft, pear-shaped organ. It's also called the *womb*. It is the place where the baby develops when a woman becomes pregnant. (More about the uterus on page 35.)

Having a period involves blood, but we're not actually bleeding when we menstruate. We're not cut anywhere. The uterus is just letting go of a special lining that it makes for itself each month. The lining is made of a small amount of blood and tissue, and that's what makes up *menstrual blood*.

Releasing menstrual blood doesn't hurt and it's not scary, as long as girls know what's going on. Sometimes, though, we can get *cramps* with our periods. Information about cramps can be found starting on page 59.

Menstrual blood dribbles out slowly over a few days (about five for most people). Then the period is over. No more menstrual blood comes out for about three or four weeks.

Then another period begins—and ends a few days later.

It takes a while for the reproductive system to get into a regular pattern, but once it does, most girls menstruate about once a month.

Not every girl or woman menstruates in a regular pattern (say, every twenty-eight days). But most do.

All women eventually stop having periods. Stopping having periods is called *menopause*. Menopause happens slowly, over many months.

The average age for stopping having periods is fifty-one.

❧ More About…the Vagina

Sometimes a girl doesn't understand where her vagina is. That's because the vagina is kind of hard to find unless you know where to look.

If you haven't found your vagina yet, you can scout it out privately next time you're getting ready for a bath or shower. You can find it by sitting down with your legs apart. It helps to use a mirror.

Your vagina is an opening into your body. It is like a soft, warm, moist passageway very close to and just below the place where urine comes out of your body. In many young girls the opening of the vagina is covered or partly covered by a fold of membrane called a *hymen*.

Every girl and woman has a vagina.

It is through the vagina that menstrual blood comes out. Girls and women catch this blood before it gets on their clothes or bedding by buying special throwaway *pads* (described on page 46) and putting them into their underwear, by using washable cloths to catch the blood, or by using *tampons* (described on page 52).

Believe it or not, the vagina is also the opening through which a baby is born.

Ouch!

How can a baby fit through an opening *that* small? This is a question many people wonder about—and a question many women ask themselves when they are about to have a baby.

The walls of the vagina are very stretchy, and during a pregnancy a woman's body goes through some changes on the inside that make it easier for the baby to come out.

Still, anybody can put two and two together to figure out that getting a baby through an opening that small is a very tight squeeze.

❀ More About . . . the Uterus

A girl's uterus is inside her body, between her *navel* (belly button) and her crotch. In young girls, the uterus is about the size of a walnut. A uterus is *expandable,* which means it can stretch—and the uterus does stretch (a lot) during pregnancy.

> The stomach is a completely different organ from the uterus. A baby does not grow in a woman's stomach. The stomach is an organ that both men and women have for digesting food. It is the place food and liquids go after we swallow.

Once a girl goes through puberty, her uterus makes a special lining every month. If a pregnancy were to occur, the lining would go through changes and become part of a system that provides nourishment and other things necessary for the development of a baby inside of its mom.

But the lining isn't needed unless a pregnancy occurs. (How a pregnancy occurs is discussed on pages 41-42.)

When not needed, the lining is released (let go) by the uterus. The lining is made of bloody tissue. Over the course of a few days the lining trickles out of the vagina as menstrual fluid.

Then the uterus begins to make a new lining all over again.

Having a period is the process of releasing the blood and tissue that lines the uterus each month.

❖ What Causes Menstruation to Begin?

As previously mentioned on page 7, hormones are the chemicals produced inside of us that are responsible for starting up and regulating the reproductive system. Besides giving signals to the body to begin growing breasts and pubic hair, hormones cause the uterus to build and then shed its lining when we have a period.

Chapter 8

❀ Here's the Scoop on ... ❀

❀ The Inside Reproductive Organs!

Some parts of the reproductive system are inside the body, and some parts are outside the body. We have already talked about two that are on the inside: the vagina and the uterus.

But there are more.

Every girl is also born with two *ovaries* inside her body. Ovaries are small oval-shaped reproductive organs located near the uterus. Ovaries contain several hundred thousand teeny unripe *ova* (eggs), each in a small sac. We are born with all of the eggs we will ever have.

Two thin tubes called *Fallopian tubes* lead from the ovaries to the inside of the uterus. The purpose of these two thin tubes—which are very, *very* close to the ovaries—is to catch eggs when they are ready and allow them to travel safely down into the uterus.

Eggs pop out one at a time. A ripened egg popping out of an ovary is called *ovulation*. Ovulation happens only in the bodies of girls who have reached puberty.

One month an egg pops out of the ovary on the left, and the next month an egg pops out of the ovary on the right.

The Fallopian tubes take turns catching the eggs.

Every egg that pops out of an ovary ends up in the uterus, regardless of which tube it travels down.

The very bottom of the uterus is considered a reproductive organ of its own. It is called the *cervix*. The center of the cervix has a small opening called the *os*. Menstrual blood dribbles out through the os when a girl or woman is having a period.

During childbirth, the os gets really wide and allows a baby to squeeze out of the uterus, through the vagina, and into the world.

The os only opens wide for a baby to come out. The rest of the time it stays practically closed.

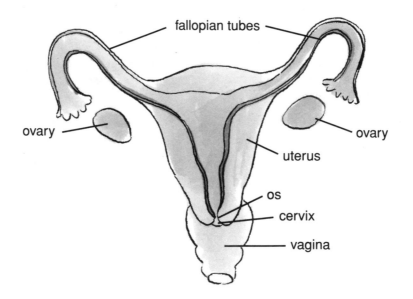

Chapter 9

❀ The Outside Reproductive Organs!

The whole group of outside reproductive organs described below has a name. It is called the *vulva*.

❀ Parts of the Vulva

A few inches below a girl's belly button is a rounded place. It's like a small hill. This rounded place is basically bald until we begin puberty. During puberty, this is where pubic hair mainly grows. The rounded place is called the *mons pubis*. We rarely use or hear this name or the other Latin names listed below. But all of the private places on our body have names, and it's not a bad idea to become familiar with them.

Below the mons pubis are two plump skin folds that come together to form a line. These are called *labia majora*.

If a girl looks very closely, she can see two smaller folds of skin that are around the openings of the vagina and the place where pee comes out. These two smaller folds also have a name: *labia minora*.

The *vestibule* refers to the area surrounded by these two smaller folds. Small glands called *vestibular glands* sometimes empty out a slippery substance into this area.

The *hymen* is the fold of skin that partially covers the opening of the vagina on some, but not all, girls.

The *clitoris* is the small, round "bump" just above the place where pee comes out. The clitoris is responsible for pleasant physical feelings.

As mentioned earlier, grownups who are in love with each other often express their loving feelings by kissing, holding, and touching each other in special ways that feel good. This "romantic" kind of touching is called *sexual touching*. It can include having *sexual intercourse*, which can lead to a woman's becoming pregnant and having a baby.

❧ The Birds and the Bees...

All living creatures *reproduce,* from the tiniest moth to the largest rhinoceros. To reproduce means to make anew or make again.

No species could continue to inhabit the earth without having the ability to reproduce.

Many living things reproduce by mating, which means that a male and a female parent contribute *genes* to their offspring. Genes carry the information needed to form new life. They are contained in the female's eggs and in the reproductive cells of a male and are *united* (joined together) during the mating process.

Putting male reproductive cells into the body of the female so that a sperm can unite with a female's egg is what mating is all about.

❀ Sexual Intercourse

Animals that reproduce by mating have special and mysterious ways of courting each other. Courtship usually comes before the act of mating. Ever seen a turkey parade around with his tail fully fanned out? He might be doing this in hopes that a female turkey will think he's so splendid that she won't be able to resist mating with him.

People court each other, too.

When we are young adults and adults, we meet and talk, get to know one another. We spend time together, doing things we like to do. We help each other and listen to each other's ideas and hopes and dreams. Perhaps we fall in love. Some of us marry and decide to have children together.

When a grown-up couple unites in the mating process, it is called having *sexual intercourse*. Sexual intercourse is when the reproductive organ of the male (the *penis*) releases male reproductive cells (called *sperm*) into the vagina of the female. As a result of this, the woman may become pregnant.

The male reproductive cells are very, **VERY** small—so small we can't even see them. They wiggle their way up from the vagina through the os into the uterus. From there they head up into the Fallopian tubes.

If an egg from the female has been released from an ovary and is in

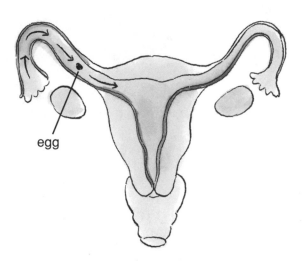

egg

the right place in a Fallopian tube, one of the male's reproductive cells will enter the egg. This is called *fertilization* or *conception*. Once one male reproductive cell enters the egg, the egg shuts all the others out.

The fertilized egg will then tumble down through the Fallopian tube into the uterus and attach itself to the lining of the uterus.

Over nine months' time this fertilized egg will go through many, many changes. It will turn into an *embryo* (the beginnings of a baby) and then into a *fetus* (an unborn baby), and then it will be born.

If the baby is a girl, she will be born with two small ovaries, two tiny Fallopian tubes, a uterus, and a vagina. Each of her ovaries will contain thousands and thousands of eggs. The eggs will not begin to ripen for many years. She will be a baby, a toddler, maybe go to preschool, and then head off to kindergarten and up through the grades of elementary school. One day, after breast buds and pubic hair and underarm hair have appeared, eggs inside her ovaries will get the signal that it's time to begin to ripen.

❁ And Then ... Ta-Da!

One of the ripened eggs will pop out of an ovary. This will be the girl's first ovulation. She won't know it when this happens, but a couple of weeks later ...

Surprise!

She will get her first period.

After that, about once a month an egg will pop out of an ovary, be caught and swept into a Fallopian tube, and will tumble down into her uterus.

Since the egg will not be fertilized, the uterus will shed its lining ... and this will happen month after month ...

... and year after year until she grows into a woman.

And it will keep on happening for about forty more years!

(She won't have a period while she's pregnant, though. See page 36.)

❁ Wondering When You Might Begin?

Each girl's body develops according to her own special timetable. This means that each of us begins to menstruate when the time is right—for us.

For some girls the time is right between the ages of eight and eleven. But for most girls a period starts later—at about age thirteen.

Does a girl's body give any clues as to when she might begin?

Sort of.

Girls begin their periods AFTER they have begun to grow breasts and

AFTER they have grown quite a bit of pubic hair. Quite a bit means an actual bunch of hairs—and not just the fuzz that first appears. Girls will have hair under their arms, too.

So don't expect to start your period when you first get breast buds or when you notice your first few pubic hairs. Your breasts and pubic hair will grow for many months before you start your period.

If you don't have breast buds or any kind of pubic hair, fuzzy or otherwise, you won't be starting your period at any time in the near future.

Still, it's helpful to know what causes menstruation to begin, how it feels, and how pads and tampons are used. It's reassuring to know in advance what to expect when you begin your first period.

✿ Here's What It Feels Like!

Menstruation feels as if a little bit of liquid is leaking out. There's no way to hold it back, so it's not like peeing. When we stand up after sitting down for a while, we often feel it coming out.

When we sit down on the toilet, it's easier for the menstrual blood to find its way out, so it does—often turning the water in the toilet pink. Sometimes during a period we see small dark red or brown clots in the water or on the toilet paper when we wipe. This is normal.

Usually there is more *flow* (how much comes out) during the first day or two of a period, and then there is less and less flow, until nothing is left but a few dribbles.

But sometimes the flow is light at first, then gets heavier, then gets light again before it stops.

❧ The Characteristics of Menstrual Blood

Menstrual blood is pink, red, rusty-colored, or even sometimes brown. Its color may change; usually it's reddest at the beginning of the period.

The menstrual blood has a smell. It's a natural odor, not at all unpleasant. But most people consider it a private sort of a smell.

When you have a period, as you change a pad you might wonder: Can anyone else smell this?

When a pad is snug up against your body inside your underwear, the smell isn't noticeable to others. If you change the pad often enough—every three or four hours or so—and take baths or showers regularly during your period, nobody will notice it but you.

When tampons are used, the odor isn't noticeable either.

Tampons are explained on page 52.

Chapter 10

❀ Pads

Many kinds of pads are made by many different companies, and they are sold at grocery stores, drugstores, and convenience stores. There are so many different kinds of pads that it can be confusing to choose which ones we want. But it's a comfort to know that they all work.

Almost all pads designed for periods have a thin layer of plastic somewhere in them to keep blood from leaking all the way through.

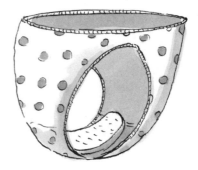

There has to be a way to keep the pad from moving around or falling out of our underwear when we walk, run, play sports, climb on the monkey bars, and generally go about our daily lives. So pads have an *adhesive strip* (a line or lines of sticky stuff) on the bottom of the pad that sticks the pad to our underwear. There's a paper strip covering the sticky stuff that we need to peel off and throw away before putting the pad on.

The pad stays stuck to our underwear until we pull it off.

Remember, the sticky side is supposed to stick to our underwear—not to us!

A pad needs changing every three or four hours, or sooner if it fills up. A used pad shouldn't be flushed down the toilet, because pads can clog up the plumbing. Roll up used pads and wrap them in toilet paper, paper towels, newspaper, or the plastic wrapper that pads often come in (you can take your fresh pad out of its wrapping and put your used pad in it). Then throw the wrapped used pad into the trash.

Panty Liners

Panty liners are basically for keeping underwear "fresh." They're not designed to hold much liquid. They can be useful at the very end of a period when we just have a few dribbles to worry about. They can also be helpful as a "backup" to catch blood that leaks down the string of a tampon. But they shouldn't be confused with *thin maxi pads,* described below.

Here are some of the kinds of pads: big, puffy ones for wearing overnight, called *overnights*; *maxi pads,* which are just good, basic pads for everyday use; *thin maxi pads,* which are very thin but still can hold a lot of menstrual blood; *slim* ones (the sides are narrow); *long* ones (for larger girls and women) and many different styles of *contoured* ones (specially shaped to fit the body). Some pads have *wings* or *tabs* (flaps with adhesive strips on them), which can be wrapped around the leg holes of underwear. Wings and tabs provide extra protection from leaking. Some pads even have Velcro strips that stick together and help hold the pad in place.

Certain pads have deodorant in them, and if they do, it will say so on the bag or box. Pads with deodorant sometimes irritate sensitive skin. They do not take the place of bathing, and they still need to be changed as often as regular pads.

Pads come in plastic bags with drawstrings or in boxes. Each bag or box has many pads in it, because we need many pads over the course of a period. In some cases the pads are in individual wrappers. These are great for carrying in a pocket, pack, or purse.

It's a very good idea for a family to keep a bag or box of maxi pads in the cupboard even before a girl starts her period, so that they will be available when she does start—and available if a guest starts her period.

New kinds of pads are being invented all the time, and they are getting better and better and easier to use—so be on the lookout for new developments!

PADS

All dads know about periods, but many aren't up on all the details because their moms and dads may not have talked to them much about periods when they were growing up. And back when your dad was a boy, boys may not have been taught that much about periods in school.

Do you live just with your dad—or stay just with your dad on weekends? If so, you may want to ask him to read this section for himself. Then he will have the inside scoop about pads, tampons, PMS, cramps, and other period stuff.

You may need him to be a pad wrangler and go to the store to buy a box of pads for you or a friend one day!

Most dads get dispatched to the store for pads at one time or another, either for a wife, friend, sister, or daughter. Choosing pads from a sea of pad choices in the grocery or drugstore may not exactly be a dad's first choice of fun things to do, but he can handle it.

If he's confused, he can be instructed to just buy *any brand of maxi pads* with adhesive strips.

AND

DADS

❖ Blood Spots on Clothes and Bedding

Almost every girl and woman winds up having to wash menstrual blood out of undies, other clothes, or bedding sooner or later. It's actually easy. Wash the spot out with a little soap (the soap in the soap dish in the bathroom will work just fine) and **COLD** water. **Remember:** Hot water will turn the blood spot into a stain, but cold water, especially if you soak the spot for a few minutes, takes the blood out almost completely—if it hasn't been there too long.

Once you've gotten the blood out of something that's washable, it can be washed along with the other laundry. But don't just throw it into the hamper when it's wet, because wet stuff packed in a laundry basket or hamper can get moldy and make the clothes around it moldy—especially in the summer, when it's hot. And mold stains are difficult, if not impossible, to get out. Instead, find a good place for it to dry before tossing it in with the other dirty clothes.

No matter how careful we are, no matter whether our pads have wings or whether we are wearing panty liners to "back up" our tampon strings, we still can get a little menstrual blood on our underwear.

Many girls and women choose not to wear their best underwear during a period.

It's true that blood washes out, but we don't always have a chance to wash it out before it stains. So we often end up having a brownish spot in our undies after they've been washed.

These clean, dry stained undies are just fine to wear. In fact, they are often the ones we choose from our drawer during our periods, because they might end up getting stained again.

❀ Bathing

When you take a bath or shower during your period, blood might come out into the water—and that's just fine. Your own menstrual blood can't hurt you in any way.

When you dry off, a little blood might get on the towel and that's okay, too. It's no big deal; it happens all the time.

Most girls and women who are menstruating prefer to dry themselves with dark-colored towels because blood can cause stains on light-colored towels, unless the towels are washed right away in cold water.

If you're visiting a friend or relative and a dark towel isn't available, it's fine to dry your body after a bath or shower with any clean towel, and then dry between your legs with toilet paper.

When you get out of a bath or shower, blood mixed with water might drip down your leg. This happens to all of us! Just dry it with your towel or use toilet paper to wipe it, or wipe it with the pad you're planning to put on.

Some of us tuck a fresh pad between our legs and kind of hold it there while we go about the business of drying off our bodies.

Tip: Don't pull off the paper covering the adhesive strip until you're ready to stick it into your undies.

> ❀ Girls and women depend on natural-born inventiveness when dealing with periods! You can, too! ❀

Chapter 11

Tampons

A tampon is an alternate way of absorbing menstrual blood. It is a small roll of absorbent material that soaks up blood in the vagina before the blood has a chance to dribble out.

A tampon is inserted directly into the opening of the vagina, usually by way of a disposable applicator.

There's a string attached to the tampon. When the tampon is full, or before four to six hours have passed, the tampon is pulled out by the string.

❖ Important Information About Tampons

If you want to use tampons, your mom, doctor, or other trusted adult can advise you as to when would be an appropriate time for you to begin. It's a good idea to wait at least several menstrual cycles before using tampons, because using a tampon can be tricky—and the safe use of tampons depends on knowing the basics of your menstrual flow.

Most girls are puzzled at first about how to use a tampon. It's helpful for a mom to explain or demonstrate.

There are detailed instructions in and/or on every tampon box. There's also a warning on every box about an illness called toxic shock syndrome (TSS). It's important to know about TSS before trying out tampons.

Tampons must be used responsibly; warnings and instructions should be completely understood.

❁ Toxic Shock Syndrome (TSS)

Toxic shock syndrome (TSS) is a very rare, but very serious, illness, in which bacterial toxins from the vagina enter a girl's or woman's bloodstream and cause her to become extremely sick—she may even die.

TSS sometimes can develop as a result of using tampons, particularly when they are used incorrectly. The symptoms of toxic shock syndrome include high fever, vomiting, diarrhea, dizziness, aching muscles, headaches, and—visible on light-skinned people—a rash that looks like sunburn. TSS begins and progresses quickly, but can usually be treated when the symptoms are noticed early.

If you have any of these symptoms while using a tampon, take it out and call a doctor immediately. Tell the doctor that you have been using tampons. If you have these symptoms while not using a tampon, still call the doctor; TSS can occasionally occur without a tampon having triggered it.

✿ The Correct Use of Tampons

Tampons come in junior, regular, and super absorbencies. To be safest, girls and women should use the least absorbent tampon that works. If juniors work, use juniors. If juniors fill up too soon to be effective, use regulars. Super-absorbent tampons are more likely to play a part in triggering toxic shock syndrome than regular or junior tampons.

If juniors and regulars leak a little, you can wear a minipad or panty liner to catch the overflow.

On days of your period when the flow is light or spotty, don't use tampons, which may be dry and scratchy. Use pads instead.

Leaving tampons in too long can trigger TSS. It's better to use pads at night while you sleep—not tampons. Girls often sleep longer than the recommended amount of time for leaving a tampon in. Besides, it's safest to alternate pad use with tampon use.

On days when you use tampons, change them regularly: every four to six hours. Don't use tampons between periods.

✿ My First Tampon Experience

When I first started my period, tampons were available, but people did-n't approve of young girls using them.

I didn't even know they existed!

The summer crowd always included some poor girl (like me, for example) who sat roasting by the pool or on the beach because she "couldn't swim." (The great big pads we used to wear were detected easily in a bathing suit.)

We had to lie to younger kids who didn't understand the meaning of the code words: "I can't swim." They'd hound us; they'd interrogate us. ("But I've seen you swim!") We'd make excuses like "Well…actually, today I just didn't feel like it."

Even though it may have been, say, ninety-five degrees in the shade.

To make matters worse, we had to worry about whether some play-ful boy (who had no older sisters to clue him in) was going to get funny and shove us into the water.

Eventually, I discovered tampons and tried to put one in. First, I briefly skimmed the how-to diagram—a cross section of the lower half of a fe-male standing sideways, which looked like a drawing of a lamb chop.

I tossed out the instructions and carefully tore the wrong end of the paper wrapping off the applicator, causing the little cardboard tubes to separate and the tampon to fall out. I had to reload it, which was no small chore.

Little did I know that I would continue to make the same mistake on a regular basis for the next ten or twenty years of my life.

Next came the hard part: getting the tampon in. At that time, the tips of the applicators weren't rounded. Ouch! I poked and pushed, then gave up; it hurt too much!

After several rounds of this, I finally learned how to insert a tampon. The secret, I discovered, was to put it in at an angle, pointing it in the direction of my tailbone, instead of straight up.

I would have learned this by studying the lamb chop drawing more carefully.

✿ Inserting a Tampon

Most tampons have an *applicator* consisting of two thin plastic or cardboard tubes that fit together. The tampon is inside the outer tube. A *removal cord* (string) hangs out of the inner tube. The inner tube acts as a plunger.

The applicator is wrapped. Hands should be washed before unwrapping a tampon so that the applicator will stay nice and clean.

When putting in a tampon, it's important to be relaxed and to be in a comfortable position—either sitting with knees apart or standing with one foot elevated (up on something, like the toilet seat, for example).

The outer tube of the tampon applicator is held with the thumb and middle finger (see diagram). It is held very close to where the inner tube meets the outer tube.

The tip of the applicator should be pointed toward the lower back. The applicator is gently pushed into the

vagina, stopping when the thumb and finger holding the outer tube touch the body. Then the inner tube is pushed in with the index finger and the tampon is released into the vagina. The whole applicator is pulled out and thrown away or flushed, if it is a flushable kind.

The tampon is left in the vagina, with the string hanging out.

When the tampon has soaked up all the blood it can, or after about four to six hours have passed, it is pulled out by the string. It is pulled out from the same angle (direction) that it was put in. Then the tampon gets wrapped up (in toilet paper) and thrown away or flushed, if it is a flushable kind.

Putting in a tampon shouldn't be painful. Turning it a little as it goes in may be helpful. Once correctly in place (in far enough) it will feel perfectly comfortable.

The opening of the vagina, in most girls, is covered partially by the hymen (a fold of mucus membrane). Occasionally, the structure of the hymen will not allow easy passage of a tampon. Usually, though, the hymen will allow passage of a tampon, particularly a slender one.

Tampons that don't have applicators are also available. These tampons are simply unwrapped and gently pushed into the vagina.

❀ Pads, Tampons, and Swimming

If we were to wear a pad when swimming, there might be a problem with blood coming off the pad into the water or dribbling down our leg when we get out of the pool. A very good thing about tampons is that with a tampon in place, it's possible to swim conveniently without worrying about all that.

What if swimming is your sport and you need to participate in a swim meet or other event and you don't choose to use a tampon? If you're on a swim team, your coach may have some ideas.

But here is one suggestion you may want to consider: Trim a thin maxi pad to fit the crotch of your suit. Have it ready to stick into your suit—but not until just before you race. In the meantime, wear a regular-size pad in your swimsuit and wear boxers or sweatpants or shorts over your suit.

Just before your event, go into the bathroom and take out the regular-size pad and throw it away. Stick the clean, trimmed pad into the crotch of your swimsuit. Stick the sticky stuff on nice and tight! Put your pants or shorts back on.

Participate in the event, then hop out of the pool and wrap a towel around your waist. As soon as you can, throw away the trimmed pad and put a fresh dry pad into the crotch of your suit. And put your shorts or pants back on.

If you have a second event, you can repeat all of this.

Chapter 12

Cramps

During a period—usually at the beginning—some girls and women experience a dull ache or pain in the lower belly or lower back. This pain is usually referred to as *cramps*. Hot baths, warm hot-water bottles, exercise, stretching, staying active, keeping busy, and thinking positively can help us deal with cramps.

But even if we have a positive attitude, cramps can make some of us feel pretty miserable at times. It may be necessary for you to *ask a parent* if you can be given some mild medicine to make the pain go away. There are medicines in the drugstore that can help relieve cramps.

Medicine that we choose off the shelves in the grocery store or drugstore is called *over-the-counter* medicine. If your parent isn't sure which over-the-counter medicine is best for you, your doctor or the *pharmacist* (the expert who works in the pharmacy section of the drugstore) can advise your parent.

Please don't take any drugs at all without first asking permission of your parent, even if you have taken the medicine before. Any drug can be harmful if someone takes too much at one time, takes it too often, or takes it while she or he is taking certain other medications.

Make sure a parent or other trusted adult supervises you when you take medicine. Don't take medicine in the dark or at night when you are sleepy. If you get cramps in the night, wake up your parent and ask for the medicine so no mistakes will happen.

Only a certain, small amount of pain medicine can be taken at one time, and it is necessary to wait the required amount of hours before taking more. You and your parent should read and follow all directions on the packaging.

It's a good idea to actually write down the time on a piece of paper when you take pain medicine. That way, you will be able to figure out what time you can safely take more pain medicine if it's needed later on.

If another girl offers you her cramp medicine, say no thanks. It may not be the right medicine for you. Only an adult should give you medicine (and only with your parent's permission).

WARNING

Do **NOT** take aspirin for cramps. Occasionally aspirin can cause a serious illness called Reye's syndrome if a child or teenager takes it when she or he has a certain kind of viral infection. Since it's possible to have a viral infection without realizing it right away, play it safe: *Don't take aspirin* or drugs containing aspirin.

✿ *What If the Pain Doesn't Go Away?*

In some cases girls and women have cramps that are so painful they need to see a doctor or other licensed health-care provider (like a nurse practitioner).

No one needs to feel extreme pain during a period.

A doctor can prescribe drugs that help manage the pain. These drugs are more complicated and stronger than over-the-counter cramp medicines, and so their use needs to be supervised by a doctor. The label on the packaging explains how the medicine should be taken. Every medicine is different, so the label must be read carefully. If there are questions, talk to the doctor's office or pharmacist *before taking the medicine*.

A health-care professional should be aware of all medicines that a person is taking before prescribing more medicine. No one should combine any medicines, including over-the-counter medicines, without checking with the doctor or pharmacist first.

✿ Contacting Your Doctor

It isn't often that we need to talk to a doctor about what's going on with a period, but sometimes it is necessary.

All serious pain should be reported to a doctor. Sometimes pain that happens during menstruation is actually not being caused by the period. It is being caused by something else that needs medical attention right away. That's why all serious pain, including serious pain in the lower belly or back, should be reported to the doctor immediately.

Periods usually last three to seven days. Heavy flow for more than a week is unusual and should be reported to a doctor.

Soaking a pad in less than an hour is unusual and should be reported to a doctor.

Bleeding between periods should be reported to a doctor.

If a girl or woman feels weak, dizzy, or faint during her period, or at any other time, this also needs to be reported to a doctor.

Women and girls—especially those with heavy periods—need to eat foods that contain iron and drink plenty of liquids. Iron can be found in leafy green vegetables, red meat, eggs, whole-grain cereals, and cereals that have iron added to them.

Many girls and women take a *multivitamin* (daily pill containing essential vitamins and minerals) that includes iron to make sure they are getting enough of it.

❖ Premenstrual Syndrome

Besides inward and outward *physical changes* (changes of the body), hormones can also cause *emotional changes* (changes involving our feelings). Hormones can cause extreme grumpiness before a period or during the first few days of a period. This is called *premenstrual syndrome,* or *PMS* for short.

Not every girl gets PMS.

Those who do might feel grouchy, sad, or generally upset just before a period or just after a period begins. Some get tender breasts and puffiness in their hands and face. Increased hunger and acne may also occur, and symptoms may vary from month to month.

PMS can result in arguing with friends, door slamming, toothbrush throwing, desperate feelings about having nothing good to wear to school, and fury over events that wouldn't otherwise be considered such a big deal.

Grown women get PMS, too. It may account for the times your mom basically blows up just because every article of clothing you own has been thrown on your bedroom floor, along with baseball mitts, the family photo album, and the fish food.

Nobody talked about PMS when I was a kid, because nobody knew about it. But looking back, I remember thinking my mom—who really, *really* loved me—hated me. About once a month.

PMS is a pain in the neck.

Some girls and women talk to their doctors and get professional help for PMS.

Chapter 13

❀ Your ❀ First Period ❀

Since no girl can tell exactly when her first period will begin, it's a very good idea to have a few pads tucked away. But do remember the clues: In almost all cases a girl will have two breasts and a patch of actual pubic hairs before she starts.

Some girls who feel like they're ready to start carry one or two wrapped pads along to school, zipped in a backpack pocket—just in case. They also take one or two along if they're going on a sleepover.

And you know what? Even before you start having periods, there's nothing wrong with wearing a pad for an hour or so—it's fine to just take one for a spin to practice up, as long as your parent doesn't mind. *Please don't experiment with tampons, though.* (See page 52.)

❀ Welcome to the Club!

When you begin your period for the first time, you will most likely notice it when you sit down to go to the bathroom. You'll see a spot, smudge, or dribble of blood in your underpants. Or you might notice when you wipe that there's some rusty or pinkish color on the toilet paper.

If you're at home, tell your mom or somebody else you feel comfortable talking to.

If you are home alone, don't worry. You can handle it. You'll know what's going on and what to expect. You might feel excited! If you feel a little nervous or upset, that's okay, too.

Most periods begin slowly, so you'll have time to set up.

If you have a "just in case" pad, get it. If it's been lost in the rubble on your closet floor or it's under your bed with half a peanut butter and jelly sandwich and a Dumbo eraser stuck to it—help yourself to another one out of the bathroom cupboard, which is where most of us have our pad stash.

A small blood spot in the underwear never hurt anybody, but if you're at home you may as well change into clean undies. You can put the ones with the blood spot into the hamper—just roll them or fold them so the blood won't get on other clothes in the hamper.

They can be dealt with later.

Or you can set them aside for a moment—and then wash them in cold water and hand soap in the bathroom sink and hang them someplace to dry.

Next, peel off the paper strip that covers the sticky stuff on the bottom of the pad. If the pad has "wings" or other tabs, there will be more than one piece of paper to pull off. But start with the paper on the pad. With your underpants on but pulled down a little, you can see what you're doing. Stick the sticky side of the pad down onto the crotch of your undies.

Give the pad a good squeeze against your undies so it gets really stuck!

THEN take care of the wings or tabs. Take off the papers. Wrap the wings or tabs around and stick them to the bottom outside of the crotch of your underwear.

We have to kind of guess where exactly is the best spot to position a pad. Every beginner has to start someplace. So just stick it right smack in the middle and pull up your underwear—it won't be far off the target!

You can check in a little while to make sure that the blood is dribbling onto the middle of the pad and not coming too close to the front or back edge of the pad. If it's coming too close to the front edge, you can unstick the pad and change its position a little, either farther to the front or farther to the back. If the sticky stuff won't stick twice, you might need to get a fresh pad.

That's all you have to do!

Usually, we need to change a pad every three or four hours.

But you might need or want one sooner.

❧ If You Don't Have a Pad…

If you don't have a pad, everything will still be just fine. Lots of things can be used for a pad in an emergency.

You can roll up some toilet paper around your hand—a bunch of it—and put it into your undies.

Or you can use a small stack of paper napkins or squares of paper towel. Fold them in half and tuck them into your underwear, like a pad. Since these homemade paper pads don't have any stickum on them, they might move around when you walk—so check often to make sure they're getting the job done.

Before pads were invented, women used clean cloths to catch the blood—and many women still do. All of us can if we need to. A wash-cloth folded in half will do as a temporary pad. Any small, absorbent, clean piece of cloth or clothing can be used as a temporary pad—even a clean sock will do in a pinch.

❧ If You're Not at Home…

If you begin your period when you're not at home, that's okay, too. Most periods begin slowly. You can tuck a big fat wad of toilet paper into your undies for the time being. Try to get a pad as soon as you can, but remember: There's no need to panic. Everything will be just fine. And periods *do* start slowly.

If you're at school, you may want to share this event with a close friend. She may even be able to help you scout out a pad.

Remember that almost every school office has pads for girls who begin their first periods—or begin any period unexpectedly. Go to the office and ask for one—or ask a teacher, librarian, school nurse, principal, teacher's aide, or school office secretary to find you a pad.

You probably won't have gotten any blood on your clothes when you first notice that your period has begun. It will most likely just be in your underwear, and it will probably be just a smudge!

But if by chance a little blood has made an appearance on shorts, skirt, dress, or pants, you can tie a sweatshirt or sweater or jacket around your waist, and nobody will know.

Remember:

Almost all women who haven't reached menopause have periods, so many of us have spare wrapped clean pads in our purses, briefcases, or packs. A female teacher probably has a box of pads in her classroom cupboard. Or there may be a pad machine in the women's restroom.

Most of us are more than happy to provide a spare pad for another woman or girl who finds herself unprepared for a period—or to provide a quarter for the pad machine.

It's kind of a girl thing!

❖ If You Begin During the Night…

If you begin your period in the middle of the night, you may wake up and discover that you've gotten some blood on your pajamas or on your sheets or blanket, but nothing will have been ruined.

Don't be afraid to wake up your parent.

You or your mom (or stepmom, foster mom, grandma—or dad, for that matter) may want to rinse the bedding, but the decision will probably be to wait until the next day to wash it.

If you start your period in the middle of the night, it's fine to just put on a pad and go back to sleep. Everything can wait till morning.

✿ STILL a Kid

Beginning to have periods is a big step toward becoming an adult woman, but only as far as the body is concerned. When a girl starts her period, someone might tell her, "You're a woman now!"

But she isn't really.

And she won't be for a long time.

A girl stays a kid the whole way through puberty and past it. Breasts, new body hair, and having a period won't change that. She'll still be a kid, entitled to the love, care, and protection of the adults around her.

❧ And So Will You

You will still be a kid.

And you will still *stay* a kid.

And you will still do all the same things you used to do. You will still act the same way you used to act. And your family will still love you the same old way.

And your parents will still boss you around.

The only difference is that for a few days each month you will be wearing a pad or tampon while you do such things as shout at your brother, eat root beer Popsicles, snuggle with Beanie Babies, and watch TV in bed—eating corn chips and getting crumbs in the sheets.

Pay attention to
your own feelings.

Curious about something? Ask questions.

Worrying about something? Talk to

your family, your teacher, or your health-care provider about anything that you're wondering about—*especially about anything that's hurting you, troubling you, confusing you, or making you feel uneasy or afraid.*

Take good care of your body.

Wear your bicycle helmet. Wear protective gear when you play sports. Wear your seat belt!

Eat well—eat lots of food that's good for you.

Don't diet unless you are being supervised by a health-care professional. Eat, play, grow, and be strong.

You're growing… and you're growing up, and there's

lots to learn. **But you've got lots of time to learn it.**

Index

About the Author

Mavis Jukes is the award-winning author of several books for children and teenagers, including the Newbery Honor Book *Like Jake and Me, No One Is Going to Nashville, Blackberries in the Dark, Getting Even, Wild Iris Bloom, I'll See You in My Dreams,* and *It's a Girl Thing: How to Stay Healthy, Safe, and in Charge.* She taught school for several years—and became a lawyer—before becoming a children's book writer. Mavis Jukes has volunteered as a juvenile defense attorney and is currently teaching leadership, writing, and human interaction in the public school system. She lives with her husband, the artist Robert Hudson, and their daughters in Sonoma County, California.